hotspur

(or, these riots and honors)

Carmen A. Aiken

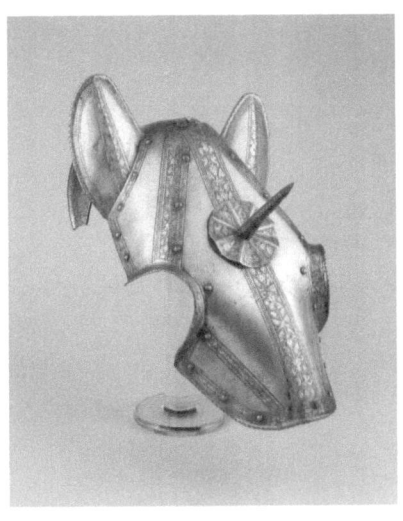

SPUYTEN DUYVIL
New York City

ISBN 978-1-963908-72-5

Library of Congress Control Number: 2025936197

[D]ivisions and insistence on places of action impose a formal and rigid structure which the play does not have.

P. H. Davison, Introduction to Henry IV Pt. 1

Don't you think alone in the mountains

Something might happen between us?

Pedro Lemebel

how little sleep
the nights, the brave, the brief

the princes that die with us
the hours, their arrivals

at ends and at paces
away from vilest earth against veins, kingdoms
the names, times, endings

the body and the boy keep not
can't contain stars

honor sparked weaker than tongues
muscles shoulders veins
bent

fortune's made minions,
little, sweet, of both
the nights, these riots and honors

throat, threat, thrust and tread,
fair rites of tenderness.

lights down

I have always wanted to be smaller. This is how you would know me, as a type of stock easy to be valorized, though few would call me common. Because it is not as though I am not in stature short, no. But that when I rush a space, there is no doubt I have shown my face. Yet. A hero is to be lean: a chest to fit in a breastplate, a stride long, and with no swollen places, a body in ease.

Through the wood. We made way. Trees older than any evidence of kings. You led us down, and we lost even the sun quickly, slipped whole to its burial, an after equinox orange that continued to bleed about us, that pricked my heart.

For I made my way through exile, I rode through exile. It wasn't so bad. Not like any harm from the battles howled through before we were fair met. An exile we could meet. You, of course, my defeat. And this? Exile.

'The purpose you undertake is dangerous;'-- why, that's
certain: 'tis dangerous to take a cold, to sleep, to/
drink; but I tell you, my lord fool, out of this/
nettle, danger, we pluck this flower,
safety.

'The
purpose you undertake is dangerous; the friends you
have named uncertain; the time itself unsorted; and/
your whole plot too light for the counterpoise of so/
great an opposition.'

Say you so, say you so?

Henry IV Part 1 III.ii.

How could I have known, little prince?
Still, it was a kingdom of ours to roam together.
Your favors and allies, my camps, my easy
loyalties, and the arms who met mine.
Mine: not easy, but how would you have known this?

for they did deny me
for there were no ladys closer,
for they loved me

for I sought swords
for I sought scars

for all and your court of scared winners,
for your empty chests,
for you were all poor little rich thieves,
or perhaps just cowards

for we knew how to ride until our end
for you called defeat before my surrender
for the prince of the kingdom
for the kingdom which will not release
like a loyalty, like a friend

for the changing shapes and space
of this defeat

one boy's rebellion, insurgence to birth
blood plus bottles fair females fires fights
a joke
of a robbery
oh how! oh revolt! pretty prince, naked
fingers thrust up, fisting clumsily, thrusting to
sanguine and law father king and country

whispers, hisses in the dark
voices dusky drunk guttural from below
the rebel, yes, the boy has yet to know.

(and some back of the envelope analysis:

some write Falstaff as breast,
the real hips bear no existence
hence, in this, thin mention

making the rest bastards, even if kind
the conquers they coax? not this country

thieves are family and who are you to say?
they fit and flesh with the line
so who is this one, here, astride?)

So you'd think me more as one's Falstaff, a Poins, Pistol, or Nym.

What, ho---
Falstaff only fucks women.

to have come from the north

to always ready for battle to fix for fights if I could not shear my soft I could
make for a lunge I was younger younger younger and drank my throat hot
climbed into barrels emerged from the spin the dark and proved proved proved
with these rowdy and unlucky down drowned with cheek drafted and hot
tongue draft after draft you see to spur is to go forward, onward but I was a
still a kid aspiring to a kingdom then and how to swallow a prince, how to
court favors, for of course I knew the heat of mine and Wales, the shore so
cold I was younger then, do not believe my big if darkened eyes, I was young
I was learning to lunge was a girl (only) not only wholly halfie then which
was the only way to be no matter barrels or fuck tongues or shorn skulls in
Wales I went to find horses and still amidst them were men and still tied to me
but still I am telling you this is about loss

How goes the adventure there why aren't you around more that boy of another
land inquired not yet stoned no means for to do, and so how the horses were:
shaggy, and with some cheer called ponies mostly the color of sand possibly
wan no smell of disobedience or cruelty, the boyfriend said Those are the
saddest ponies I've ever seen, how the man was: pale but every son I met on
that island was and now I see a man his boy's grin teeth intact, a bite of a
smile and slammed onto him sweaty bony all I knew of how men were then
aggression in his eyes easy to separate him from his phalanx teeth more than
tongue, lips, even the field too human it had rained all day the French defeated
all howling songs of why, why, why! the pain and dry skull split the winged
heavy wait my fist hauled away when the others realized I'd gone down

didn't go to button up they beat me to retreat I was gonna I explained, outside
the snow started later we would march to the sea cold cliffs trying to pretend
there were no new worlds Who are you anymore I don't even know what to
say to you but by the time that night came and went how could I not learned

how to take those parts of me and lose them from days see I have never understood the need to speak all the keep so said The ponies are shaggy here and we all got drunk, and years and years gone those who rode with me having courted and found fortune and long gone I would forget the man who didn't go to make his own shut neat retreat I told my courting friends the banishment the abdication the plot's defeat remained inevitable for a hundred reasons, but not that.

The Rumors

--- boy, it's not good: the murmur
murder, and remember
that king, a revered sweet
a son in constant stumble, retreat

See the King's blood,
not in boil or slouch
in halls after taking leave
weakness for drink
But pale, bleaked, flinched
quick at swords of rumor

could be chain rustle
or wind
or words of rebellion

hotspur, prince

Claims come from below and
the feathered king's blood drains, dregs
sorcerer storms, Welsh rage. The scald.

Chills: this is the North, it's dissolved dawn discoveries
vein-kept knowledge of these changelings.
Coincidence in riotousness, alienation,
keen ears, codes, questions.

Inglories, constant
this chosen, this honored
this mouth traitorous as rival blood.

Which lines to cut yet not hemorrhage, but fade
which curses to condone, swipes to blink away

Which strings, silver pieces eke survival, ignore stupor
which lines to send
which coax aside blood

When what warrants return?
Fields, flags, stone

which is to mean
the oblige of death.

The Friends You Have Named Uncertain

A family's no more than a land tied set anyway, instead try and believe
domestique could mean prestige, or named nobility for those providing care
(soigneur, liege, not tu mere), so let us say:

to feed off to thieve off to scratch at to fall
into ending up with the carekeeps who nourish the shoulders who bail
the captains who fade the boys who eye, swallow, rise:
one always rises or takes off, away.

Call it what you will - so few, these few
these happy few - something to teach
to convince the believing, the loved
they'll lose.

once more to the

What is a mortal wound?

For the ground gained, for each victory which must be as
thrill, release, as exhalation, collapse--

and as you'll know, and by my troth,
love a joke, and not a fucking jock.

But a squire of the night's body though
not known to be tame and oh,

                              the things I will court

Say I: there's a land farther beyond denial of desire, the quiet keen
of hope to possibility, the defeat.

No cavalry, no loyalty. The notches and medals
and then there is the absence
defeat and surrender, varieties of exile.

If a mortal wound is only a one marring
our days until their end, who can know?
The odds ended up against me, which is to say,
they were easy odds. Even if this starts early,
molars rancid with acid, brands at the calves,
these never amount to the wars

                              O, gentlemen, let us limit
                              ourselves to these scenes

No divide, why insist?
None of this is formal, and hard is
not the same as rigid

Well. Still. The directive:
Hotspur, mortally wounded.

> O, gentle, never fear
> it was not just you
> who robbed me of my youth

God help thee. Come, say there are two scenes:
Hotspur, in defeat as the years go by, as a Prince plays his fields,
his days, the notes inline with a directive of birth, of ascent.

This youth, its heart, anon, go on
And ask this from these bodies
how a wound will open you until your end.

And that same sword-and-buckler Prince of Wales,
But that I think his father loves him not
And would be glad he met with some mischance,

Henry IV Part 1, I.iii.

some mischance

to the east, spires, and then in both directions about the coast. aha, cute,
let's swap: there is a Prince from the north and a warrior from the south.
still. later.

begin with one: the terrace warm and the night, too, and still the outside
in its noise and the motion of people, the trees, the earth, well. these, the
substantive state. hotspur, even in motion, knows this is peacetime. that
war has been gone these good months. the wound. their prisoner's body
full and their skin is burnished and their hair grown in, their mouth - the
matter of the skull will always be coming, the skull comes later.

hotspur moves in quiet, this is how to be. and the ladies walking loops,
arm-in-arm with them to beer and table, and the sun level with the edge of
the parapet. hotspur is in neutral court and smiles, carefully.

(we do not always enter, so:)
Ha, says the Prince. hotspur, right?

nothing like rare accidents

How easy to blaze at night,
how to know to make the eyes bright,
the rest turnt away then know
you've won. And the sun to
incinerate a wake and how to know the dark without the burn?
Amidst the second betwixt spark and crash
we find the line of a hand, the jaw's stab.
        By how much better than my word am I?
by what, depth and width and weight and height?
No, cannot love and give in the first five or ten grins.
Wait weeks, hangovers, sweetness' shallows.
Worsen the tonguing, see who follows.
        Your fathers stay old, so do your kings.
Steeds lost, their fucks gone to queens,
standing on sullen shoulders, and yours,
planted there into debted ground.

[Some Mischance]

Blue skin. Almost. Quiet approach. A back's starved bird. No albatross, sleeker, less rigid than crane or heron. A vain winged chest: an undoing: a breastplate of span beyond bruise. Almost settles, then perches. Shadow quick presses against blades, no shoulders. Hotspur: meets the chill press against twice, twice twice, twice four, then

[Re-enter Eastcheap:]

Behind. Hotspur, swollen front. Without drink without bounce back heat between hearth and drunk company gathered sweat of shirt in strain and stain for days without any and all Hotspur burns, the blood surely steams. The heat and Hal with barely a recoil. A flaw. Not fatal.

--my bed you've taken.
Ah, but I've paid for it--

Something keeps the rebel press dry. Dust and road settled between skin cell and sheath. Catch the hands pulled to worked jaw. Look. Red ravines from rein embrace. Impossible practiced soft to calloused pale. Hal: wonders cold blood, wrong and escaping to touch, stale, spent. Feet lined up at bed's end. Boots. The bay glint hair scalds out of Hotspur above Hal, dark. Embered smile, suggestion. Closed, biding.

--long night, understand
oh, you do now
this is where night ends---

Hazel glint, Hotspur, green, in subdue, too. Noble if barely deep. Reflect up stained leg, belt. Catch. Fine enough brown where at pupil embrace dissolves alchemy. Blue eys. Pretty, expanding. Carried above violet

washes, lined distinction, maybe, yes. Eyes whose only trust is loss.
Neither blink.

boy this chivalry.
sir, I live with my deeds

A thousand fights coil and splinter spaces of hands, impacts, stings,
embraces, absence. First spark shift of flank, yank, laugh cast hands
about the walls about the bodies, the fields so far away from them,
beyond. Oh. They do understand.

bit of a small field
stay or what you will

The charge. Fighting dirty. Only flint iris to neck. Bite. A bite. Bitten.
Before the blood blossoms between lateral wall of neck Hotspur
realizes. Legs go for the middle to bellow but regains yanks arm to
slender shoulder palisade shoves hard. Groan and gratifying surprise
and noted shiny incisor still bared, this fine breeding. Blue grinning
barely beards caught in stretch, smile. Straw pricks rustles stirs. Pricks
stir. Sticky turn, reel to corner elbows to the sternum, bruise near the
heart. Click counterpart to a nicker.

where will all your honor get you?
mine
and?

Winged joint to lean arm stumbles into the hold latch and wither
of Hotspur. Shifts to the wall the drunken hearth the skin of the
pomegranate's chamber. Locked. Pinned. Quick breaths shallows slows
hazel flint swivel swipes on burnt cheek. Against the wall. Pause.
Detente no another dirty trick. Wild colt, spine rearing and tailbone

and ass. Laughs! and laughs. Too late. Cinch of broad hands trap the
slim forearms still. Power, top or bottom, and aversions to surrender
but a squirm stifled as the rope of wrist goes so tight the possibility of
trapped lungs comes into question. Staying is secure.

fuck

Slippery little fuck. Beat skinny for rejoinders. Tries again to buck
only the game shrinks, the circle tightens. Bucks, though, and bucks,
no bridle, snaps as though to find one, the air swollen with friction.
Choose. Reckless. Leaps in, no, not the first of these riots. Clamps to
draw skin poker tongue to bite, burn.

fuck

In this bite the cold skin like drawing on hand cupped water it is
warm between lips it is dissolving on the tongue it is thin and lean
and it will not give it is smooth and blue and it will not break it is the
cold yeast inhale of ale and salt of fights and bent leather well treated
and well kept it is protected and precious between the fronts of his
teeth and the brush of skin below the lip. In bite the clenched bird boy
skin cries to blood and blue and pulls taut, only in the second until
it leans to groan. Thaws. Moans. Here in the body of this prince cells
warm pushing the skin closer to the source heat, pull and orbit, they
push back to the comet of Hotspur. To bite and burn this is the knees
hitting the dirt this is the ring of blades on the earth. In this bite is the
end to fight, the turn.

fuck

They fuck. They are fucking. They fuck, the word a place between
and about and beneath fight and fondle and fool and fall and finish

and freak and fellate and find. There is no other word. They make no
love and no amend, not stillness and space together. Something shared
but not cherished. Something earned but not treasured. Something
kept but not held. The field crouched at the walls the dry wind hisses
slid by ears and out throat. Soft river in hands, trained holds. Steps, as
hooves can dance, graceless sharing. Jerking. Slippery fingers in sliding
locks. Dark like water and dirty, the pull of barley between fingers.
Harness head up to breathe away, the rolling irises, chapped lips.
Snapping. Releases the mane and the boy whirls back, perched between
pommeled symphysis, deep keep of hipbones.

fuck

Riding, rides, hide and cloth able to smoke were there flame for buckle,
the heat dry. Burnt press of lip. Not a kiss. They are drawing their
swords they are sparring and testing will. Mounted. Prince ascended,
atop, cub, colt, buck. Clenching and riding without thought of throw
the throw the thud the face down to the ground. Trusts the lead the
lead back easy unconscious gratitude of lean haunches, grace in an ass.
Up. Down. Up. Down. Up. Down. And almost molded holding them
together and bearing down begging to be thrown to beat hard a trot
to a canter to a gallop a reckless rider pushing could drag them both
down to spark the straw to tumble in collapsed bones on the stones
only they'll vault the walls and the bars and the beams and stars and
field and wind they'll vault glory and pride and reticence and renown
and peace and praise and safety and grace and dignity and honor and
chivalry and duty and blood and the pace too much too much the
saddle almost slicked off rubbed out clothed legs bare backed cavalry
too much to carry the weight will lose the legs over shoot stumble let
the load loose blow them to disgrace---

fuck

Kindness, then, body's sweet technique, and gratitude Hotspur harder
allows sinew to still blood and bareback boy Hal takes the long veins
like water runs over coarse wrist forearm and finger once, twice, soft
touches, tap and sibilant sign leads him leads them pleads for the turn
the lean arm lifted and halted to the steady ground static bed given
stability of stones each peeling off they are beyond men still in spur
and mount take the land at a gallop tack vanished unwilling to spook.
Undoing. Belts buckles tugs shrugging leather arms around necks as
bridle, nose to mouth sweet as a shank relaxes the hips in braces the
wall slow gait stamp, stamps, pulls at belt, in the air. Eases. Rears, down
easy, once, down easy, twice, down, down.

fuck

They are fucking. This accord, the scent of them thick enough to
alight. Pulled cock grip gives in. The fucking that is fighting that makes
centaurs the thieving and battle lusty blazing through the temples and
the thighs fills fauns of thirst swollen so fierce to carve horns. The clash
of horns of beasts and boys left behind belts on bones snap of leather to
skin. The cries and snorts, sighs and groans of gaits and flanks and legs
sliding between stallions ready to mount. They will bleed on the trees,
make them lean, those that bleed that come that fall in soaking backs
bare flesh breathing hard and hides wet.

Let each man do his best:

Henry IV Part 1, *V*.ii.

not that these are good words they are a good many words good
these good many words this mouth judge this judge this tongue
from the words know the red howl the wet muscle opening the
ache of open jaw which is ferocity for there are those who die
by words there are those who kill for words there are those their
words burn into ember dissipate to ash to the ground to wash to
runoff the creeks the hills the shore the sea to up and up and up
and beyond those whose blood creeps across teeth leak with the
remember to save the words to calm the throat words as blows
but mine says hope to diminish in rein then rear they then catch
at blade at wounds then ache to groan the stretched sinew, split
bones

they call me hero a word of swords, horses, hilt, pommels saddles
shields objects not honor a word not to claim to know can only
say words are not memory not fear not strength not hope here
known for both the action the reaction the mouth hot, spurred
to know at end just action not words action for words are not
often possible

the possible: the motion to hero to fight to hero the word to spur
what vaulted this body a body to man and horse to man and
sword to warrior to hero to spur and rear so easy to fall

in mornings remained stroke and curry both horse and hair and
her and both burnished my lady calls both each fine centaur
brethren of pooled eyes gleaned hair of shine even coarse no
lady closer a good woman this horse woman her lips blessing
shoulder plates and musked flanks on her and carry dust and

road a sweetness in tongue and smoke and warmth that cannot be assigned.

not the first horse how well to know no fight without a run to carry the thrum of heat twin fears of tumble and embrace of ground the tale is this voice is hot and runs a mouth when it should close but who knows the dips lulls lows not to be imitated nor thrown a boy skinny to this brawn first foal and never lost love for quick endless limbs beating blue black transparent ligament dappled iris they shine twilight black almost blood never a love of courts, their false fields, dark stone soft chill and gasped exhale those words the exchanges

took outside brushed the foals fine hair and traced a web of arteries a bone the swollen lines in the shape of hooves broad span of hard hips as strong as the backs without saddle how to learn to always watch steps know eyes know fear know feet their own possibilities of collapse to ground to soothe low and slow know those who carry you offer backs hear all only said in murmurs started below bottom the beneath the throat heart lungs how they know fear the maybe the only choice to swallow to hide to rear to accept to draw on pain to release all that might spook in the journey to ventricles to panic before ever the hope to mount the learning of the twitches in ear smell of hand near mouth the soft between teeth the learning by the tug on mane then rope then bridle how always will there be blood from fingers and lips before the faith in leather

we are men from the north and this must come to the movement from boy and pony to man and horse and men and swords the descent under dark took the walls the yeomen the women took flint to any tinder pile of certainties learned words don't work cannot save things like women's bodies or fields or throats hacked as blackthorns how as they tore at the stables and running open jawed and handed for the grain pulling at the pony learned my cry his recognition of my word was the betrayal the moment the man needed to connect to take his hilt to the star between slam slit the colt's throat escaped steam stained the night thick drip the dizzy boy slump to the field in tangled hoof and ash

now is why only the lady and strangers call to me Harry Harry Harry Hotspur for I took the sword the scalding hilt from the blaze and dark and press of bodies of men the blade a silver nitrate of the dark and ran and ran and swung to the man's laughing back hacked through his ribs drew a line to his waist he turned to this body this boy of me hand for this neck until the final slice pushed skin and bone his mouth without words the slack to groan then buckle the blood from his tongue to the colt's field

almost dawn they fled left the horses gathered our follow to their camp their left mothers and babes called honor to let the blank hollow faces trickle to the limbs of trees after the return after the crimson faced stable master pointed to a swollen bay waiting to be led back his hand placed fingers to the thick underbelly to the folded joints bare beat shuddering within her chest nodded stumbled to bury his wife the mare swelled and me sleeping next to the colt curled in her after a thaw her throwing her nostrils screeched her eyes rolled her blank tongue a birth without words without teeth for syllables only the motion of lips only a kid born on a windless night turned at birth hooves first head towards a wild heart after honor again to smash her skull not rend the belly open to let all the pastures and canters drain out as so many had dribbled before found the split between ribs forearms to release the yearling's limbs of wet cloth rubbed the neck blew on ears to remind him of breath carried him called him nothing for names are nothing I am called for my temper and my blood my rushes and reactions in years he grew never gelded no matter how they say they cannot be trusted it can be believed but trust best left to words which how to believe bonds from the throat the grasping knuckles bob of wrists and slicks of teeth all it is the seconds and hisses of breath clench between ribs and thighs the back and forth shifts of pressure weight girth air between or no his legs and mine can only hold then charge we both go down together

I by thee have watch'd,
And heard thee murmur tales of iron wars;
Speak terms of manage to thy bounding steed;
Cry 'Courage! to the field!'

And thou hast talk'd
Of sallies and retires, of trenches, tents,
Of palisadoes, frontiers, parapets,
Of basilisks, of cannon, culverin,
Of prisoners' ransom and of soldiers slain,

And all the currents of a heady fight.

Henry IV Part 1, II.iii.

liege-

Followed, always followed, a love at a four-beat and our pace almost set.
Unmatched. Care limitless, immeasurable between hearth, home, our sign
posts, the miles and time, and caught in the same hands of the carriers or
satchel of the messenger.
And this urgency from these fingers, to the sting, your hands on haunches.
These: our sounds, we know the echo, the stretch between the raise of wrist,
the tension of tendon, the strike and spur forward.

liege-

No world for small movements. Your world thus our world.
I, no lady closer, no one and no war and will not be your battle
or fight or comrade, for no lady. Closer. What of soldier? Intimate?
Arm, grip, reach? Cannot be those things, no matter the fever heat
scalding our bed, clammy now: I wake after you have left.
No, will not be battleaxe nor mace, no matter the thick grip of hands
to wrists, nor twists, nor kicks, nor clenches, nor shaking, sleep, none
closer to your retreat, this surrender, your curl of boy in the night,
holding,
a press for dear life.

liege-

burn a sun a bobbing orb these words a moon that curves to watch
stays steady on your back to watch

you the syllables that never catch you carriers with news that start
or stop blood how well I know your fast

tongue how well I know your furious and steady palm how my
words bounce, shield, coax next to the

saddle always carried always carried shouldered engraved blotted
out

always moving like this can never settle

liege-

Not just the horse:
The legs that carry you away the nails the bite
the kiss the pommel the cold rising off the hills
the echo between the walls the frail breath of women
the straw the prick the barren chest of the hearth
the supple skin of mounting the smooth spine settling
the smell the heat the hotblood the sparks lit from
the hands that carry you away the promise of
the men that carry you away the promise of
the glory
the deeds
endless
that carry you away.

liege-

What you do not know,

You fall and I fall: here I am walking. I am put to pasture.
I am watching them carry the words and paper and syllables, what
parts I am left back. I am watching the carrier turn the corner: you
fall and I fall.

Fall they say she crumbled she a clubbed mare. An all collapse,
not even a hole for the blood to drain from, never one for the
prowess of wounds. Just an absence near the heart.

I fall, and the stillness, the quiet swells, but I hollow the
marrow to the road the sweat and saliva
to the grass.

There the taste of earth: not iron, not your nimble and slick
tongue, scratched lips, the dullness seeping from the ground, an
empty taste, a mouthful of copper, the cold taste, a burnt blue taste
from a warned sky, the horns off the parapets.

They'd report: they found the rider fallen, empty as
hollowed bones, a soaking mare. She has not cried; at nights, there
comes a cry from the pastures,wet and enraged. We expect to find
the herd broken, lost to flight, but still they stand. They'd tell you I
had fallen.

But you have gone and the words rot nowhere

liege-

A boy and his horse, a boy and his whore.
Dear bonny boy, his filly and foal.
Remember your lady--
Remember thighs and flanks are not so far apart,
a kiss
as good
as a siege tower--
no, the clatter
of hooves near
the castle walls--
no, the clatter of hooves at the bedroom door.
Sweet, boy,
I dream centaur boys,
colt-legged queers.
They look like princes.
They ride like you.
Remember how I loved them before you,
how I loved,
before you.

once more

You led us through the columns of trees and though I was small, I am sure I willed to be smaller. Which was not a part of your conquer, for just a mortal wound, not surrender. Yet here we were through the trees, my hero's visage you wanted, the legs and flanks of a warrior. I handled a sword like no other. I knew riding. I took blades till their hilt.

Still I remained too full. I do not think you knew then of how I tried to, how I kept myself, for if no armor would keep my chest, I would bind myself to myself. I thought of what it would be like to move through the world with less weight, something I have carried since I stopped being a child. Since I have known I will always defend myself because I will always own what some desire. What you desired. Once.

I wept at the sea that day. I left you to the work of the fortunate, of the autonomous. At the sea I considered where exile would bring me and I wept, because I was still alive, because I would keep living. I wept because I had you there, but the die had been cast. Alea iacta est.

A hero, too, is an object of desire. If I were taller my chest would be heroic, maybe. It was a renaissance at best. Of no god or titan or nymph that I could see. I wondered if men dreamt of becoming centaurs for what their new haunches would bring. What could my transformation be? Trade this chest for wings? Had I set of hooves, would all of me be easier to bolt with? It would not be much of a loss at all.

THE FIELDS OF HOTSPUR

There are the lost: lands to their sires, their lines, their
grandfathers. The brethren, the kin: there is a noose in
a closet, there is oxycontin

There is the body to endure: the scrape out of blood,
compressed chest, or not enough years to run without
the exhaustion of the set of breasts, how burning
feels on an ankle bone, fists in the middle, spike heel
strength, light to chase, bearing weight

There are the attacks in the night: language plundered
and mourned, barricades battered and rammed, what's
to say? the common battles borne

There is the imprisonment: teeth kicked in, swollen
sleep and endless awake, and only reality's cracked
window to know what is free, their fortune to keep:
and of this tale, hotspur does not speak.

There are the men: pompous and stupid, to keep what's
their's, to threaten, to pretend, to ride behind and wait
for the front to fall and take and take, who hotspur
would deny deny deny any kindness, whose defeat
would not be enough, only ruin

How else will a warrior glitter off the foil?
How else will a warrior ride to their meet?
How else to be emptied completely
of the last moments
of youth's hope?

of this young percy's pride

hotspur, who has been overcome

hotspur, who knows a lady's love
is gold, who cannot help
the burn from a kind of combat

hotspur - to - men, the blow's contact

hotspur, who is loyal in
action betrayal compassion in
plan creation execution in
instinct impulse initiation in
activation submission release in
surrender defeat exile
(that is the order)

for fealty is a state
fealty like the chamber of a heart

Whom do I love?
Find for to whom I will carry a hope

Who are you and whom do you love?
I just want to fight everyone

A Variety of Exile

it's like the drop but worse the drop so much worse than the fall
because its just you i've faced down armies of
& you had made the momentum and power
                    the pleasure
& like that you let it be taken
                    all at once from you
& how was it possible
                    to do that?

what is hotspur without being cavalry?
being bound to hotspur

little lonely hotspur still knows how to smile
how to make an offering, pay a beauty's mind

little lonely hotspur bares a back for
a lady's charm holds fast, and lifts their arms

little lonely hotspur, hello to her attack
surrendered in the first, now free below sweet lash

Find me a rider and I will ride astride, horn, or none
have drunk pommel or elegant, sturdy curve
have kept crops to stay atop
tell the rider to know their stance.

Find me a rider and I will walk forward, a tether
to them, will not balk at nerves, quiet, or chatter
stop at any moment, stay calm
clear the way forward.

Find me a rider and I will stay
at the rear, wary, await, I will
choose to catch up or choose to stay
choose to bolt, see what remains.

Find me a rider and I will show
the bare of my back, find me a rider
unafraid, to be bare, to bear
for it is not as simple as it looks, until it is.

Find me a rider to ride aside, and I
will make a proper pair of me
a balance, clasped, ready to fall.

Once I was as a prince, once royal,
my desire determined, my favors
violet, my stable
kept to show my strength, my fit
my place in this
(or, at least, a low marquess
with a need to remind the whole of the land
my place in the arrangement of things)

Once I was a prince as I excelled
at the swift leap between worlds
eyes like copper coins, whistling out
affection, fascination, and my loyalty
well.

Which is to say, I know why
in these worlds
we return to the doors we know
we trade our names.

not an eye
But is a-weary of thy common sight,
Save mine, which hath desired to see thee more;
Which now doth that I would not have it do,
Make blind itself with foolish tenderness.

Henry IV Part 1, III.ii.

They made camp by the river, in bitter pursuit of the sun,
the day so cold. One of them from the north, one just on a constant
horizon, a knowledge of the horizontal, a latitude, wondering how
hard to fight to try and land on any single one of them. The sun arrived
for them as they passed through towns, and as they worked their way
through the countryside, so the people appeared. They continued on,
and here Hal shone in his strengths for Hotspur.

On & on they rode, began in snow and the rustle of barely
vanished winter and Hotspur, of so much of the South, bristled at
the high trail, their steeds heavy with supplies for their travails.
Then: too nervous, then struck and thick with fear and frustration
and Hal coaxing, hefting, easing the descent, and then Hotspur
watched, enthralled and thrilled when Hal took the open clean smooth
switchback, swift and giddy, and Hotspur wary but shallow-chested
with joy to see Hal float above the steed, shoulders cast back into the
afternoon's sunlight.

They camped by the river and men from the town passed by in
a truck and honked. Hotspur quiet, instinctively made eyes big, but the
truck smiled, wheezed, on its way out. By the river they tried to find
protection from the wind, with softened dirt to sleep, with the trees and
a pot to piss in within reach.

They undid their bags at the river beneath the trees and tried
to finally get a fire lit in a wind that came from all sides. The equinox
would just arrive as they finished the journey, their decamp in a
quiet Hotspur knew would be a part of the end, after held quick to
Hal's splayed legs, fingers idly engaging and Hotspur's lazy and loose
keening bit in, and then the expanse of the field of months, of the long
ends, the back, forths.

But then: by the river. The night fallen in a quick descent, and
they huddled over their bowls, threw waves at passing men laughing
and jubilant. What would they have done? Hotspur wondered. The
men kept their speed and galloped off, horns fading into the wood.

How it was so cold. They were heroes. It was almost a land Hotspur had grown on, had known, and they held so little knowledge there. They were alone, together. They could be anyone. They were strangers.

What would've happened if the winter had not chased them in the night? A small fire and the easy company of each other. A small wind to push them together. A river unfrozen and murmuring next to them, their rivers from bone and fold and blood to mouth, the depths. But, as princes are born on mornings full of lightning, as heroes are mostly curses, how could we have known any of the forces? A storm born on a sea, or as Hotspur thought and over again, you and your fucking terrible timing.

The night by the river gone so cold. They huddled and shivered and the moon rose between the trees. Hotspur, always exhausted, carrying the weight where Hal leapt from it, descending, gone. Then Hal shook and had not enough, never enough, and Hotspur cast their burly shoulders forward, kept him tight. Cried and cried. Hal was crying and crying.

It's ok it's ok it's ok it's ok, Hotspur thrummed, I love you I love you. Poured as much warmth out, imagined they could have their limbs be a warm river, their heart a cave of flame.

Hal quieted and stilled, still shook, cold.

Let me tell you a story, prince. Muse, oh muse. Hotspur tried to remember the trials, how will we ever be heroes, how will you realize your home, how will I escape the endless suck of hand on throat and how to pull him up, the rocks of loyalty to shear you to the endless. Heroes, heroes. Hotspur whispered. I'm sorry I can't tell you how we get to the end. And Hal quiet, slept, gone cold, gone into himself, the retreat.

esperance

intake, took, hail, breath
        a ready hope
        filled

comforte

taken in, dark, deep, sweet

oh my keep, once more to
the breach

once more
once more

please

a day, as in all the day, mastering
the quarters or these days, a coordinator
and now every day is cold and all hotspur
can do is pull to their skull the way
a road lines an ocean, and do they remember
and what will happen when they learn again
and anyway realizes, finally able to ride again,
sun and bare arms and wandering

where is the metaphor of desperation
for loyalty, for the acknowledgement of tame.
and where is the metaphor for the abdication after.

air, but not so. or on and on
anon and on and on, her, too, depending
a room sucked of it or lungs, or ribs
a false step

go, go, to be charged to roar,
holding fast to useless oars
amidst waves never to abate,
tides turned, still gathering rope
to lash limbs to some cliff
to offer, to stay, eyes above
the charge, bones planted
blood, not air.

no salve for a wound
where the remainder of love
continues to flow, a question
of its likeness to blood, its finiteness

for I will ease my heart,
Albeit I make a hazard of my head.

Henry IV Part 1, I.iii.

and what can I say except I watched I was young and I kept my keep by keeping the rest and at night I kept watch and I say this even as there was no fight but a need for me to sit the nights leaned on the wall the pull of smoke anger I needed to burn off the love of absence this is to say there is no blank for you to fill in this is mine no opening for you to breach to say how I have parted arms only to hold them this I keep those were bottles of ache and animal I have consumed love to anger when there is loss of self and love again this was my watch these were not the wars

there is so much to say and swallow breathe and take without words or paper drum flute map arrow blasons bloodlines land borders built and crossed here there how to say surrender retreat to pull that from a blow to the chest and the shine and strain of a day of running the silence swallowed that will not run at the stop groan of muscle in static night presing about when all is the remembrance of warmth at a back the fit of a hand breaths echoed for miles shifts of fields as though close breaths and even now this is not remembering

these are words to fill movement to create breach where otherwise there is solely smoke and dust burn of iron into flesh eyes never to catch a broad back only for a gallop a way away do these words do these dead these bleeding houses necks crumbled cinder of the barn the mothers buried embered hips and thighs to dirt do these make words of warrior of hero? they are only words and easy to lose to forget to fear at end why I ran to the smoke to the smell of foal blood why I have a lady who holds to thighs as good as I why a sword is a man's through its hard throb memory in palm and fist.

why I speak not good just many why my chest burns takes me to the fire to the sparks between blows to riding at the edges of dark why I fear my feet the fields the ground must stay atop must clench and spur hold the rear buck forward for these are words and as they blow out t spew them as ember as tinder they may catch ignite and they are lost to me letters so easy to lose not a real fear as disgrace shame and turn them and form them to lose them here it is warrior here hero here a man and his horse a man and his sword fear and remembering that and what else and nothing to lose here so run, mount, nothing left to turn back to and this we call courage this we call bravery this we call honor this we call trust this we call duty this we call loyalty this we call glory.

only how empty my palm when the weight held in lines falls from me, how cold how free

only how hard the earth in the tangle of arms that makes loss the stumble and embrace of fall

for defeat and loss become beyond what can be put to words -- and how useless -- at end we will all fall all the rest fled no lady mother father lover hands empty a burden to the earth words unable to call any of it back tongue straining to dirt and still call all of us strong

thank him,

that he cuts me from my tale,

For I profess not talking; only this--

Henry IV Part 1, V.ii.

if the flight is question
count the fights,
enough in a lifetime before mine

Disappearance is never questions of miles between
absent directions, lack of map
Rage and long thoughts crossing the fields and roads

Crows who shrug the news from home
that never really changes.

[ONLY THIS]

Window eclipse. Booted calves smelling of powder Hotspur sliding
through. Room reek of wine stale smoke a tang of metal or clavicle
sweat or bites. How lean Hal sprawled on the pallet the eyes
reserved, he chill of water evening behind Hotspur in the window
balancing.

-like smoke
The land's aflame.
believe when I say I don't care-
'

Without lines still pale and hollowed listless Yes listless Hotspur
drops down feels the chill inhales the dank spread of hair Yes.

-heard battle's like birth, heard to make the field a playing day
Hell
snorting and screaming and who gives a fuck about the women anyway
yes Often-

Softens hand on the starling back-

Often. You don't have heirs do you sir?
some foals, colts. Boys. Just-

Faint smile a pretty ear a tart clover in the curves and sweeps of
cartilage catching on Hotspur's teeth an ache Hal an ache spread to
the room and out. A chill smoke over the hills the stretch to court
the lick of the waves an expectation.

- kill your father.
think I couldn't

take the country.
syours
and me? What would you do to me?

A prince unfolds to crouched hunch and stretches, lays arms out and eyes straight to Hotspur. Catching, Clash. Hotspur beside rubs the noble back yielding in the shiver yielding in the warmth. Astride down bent to breathe in the liquor and stone the steel of crowns the bends the blows the miles

I do I will

The veins the feathers the straw the walls hands beneath shirt the slow ebb and lap beneath quickens swallows hand over hilt, slick fingers, ready for the breach, the press forward, the white light of Hotspur's hands, blaze,,and Hal's sweetness all about, all about. Arches turn mouth at neck pierce to the clavicle, marrow taste whimpers at the blood and pushes, pushes, sparks between bodies catching giving all giving none until burn and fall.

You do.
I do. I do. I do. I do. You will.

a variety of exile

so what if we are, my lord?
this is a shore with no desire, owner, end
and we bathe in the deep run the water
hot so in the dawn when I
ride off, I will have left myself
behind and we fold into each other, I
to you your tack hilt to sword, I find you,
no need for a report

You won't carry
    a weapon

you want
nothing to do
with them

when we carry swords
they hang from our hilts

my breasts do not
protect me
my chest of course
is only for others
an offering

so you see, we
both carry
I know it has been
your offering

after you left
this breach
the weight of this
sweet
of what you could not keep
a slow leak
a dissolving breach

what to do
with me?

once more, once more

HOTSPUR is wounded, and falls

And after

Less than seconds flap away
from the draining body slowly
sliding blood out of slow lips.

Boy you have crow's eyes

The black birds clacking
to the vacancy of voice, remaining
traces of hot metal smells
of away, sweet, ready for
puncture, slip, spill.

Eyes shiny as dimes
in the skull. Deep. Insolent
but without the deft tongue
darting past lips to tug
towards throat.

wound, violet
that pain, the one to end things
the wash the color
of before dark falls
the relief that will not
sweep over, in
somehow sweeter
a horizon violet, violent
night never coming on.

these princes that die with us

You my first body the field we can't quantify the cells left behind that shed off dead to make beats to beat thrust parry feint slack jack off don't believe we too thieves you're my youth my yours body your mine lifted and stolen too how many bodies in a country skulls in the field to dissolve to chalk dying gauls all that build the hills of this one those soon to be buried beneath these and my hooves your body will only feed this country only so far can we conquer bare back some women are nations lands states guarded without armies languages without arms corps the body where are the words for these exquisite corpses couldn't heft you then and will not bend bow beneath your fallow fields now at the end lay you down this is where to learn honor first to bear down on the earth conquer and lay making land breaking both the living and the dead

ill-weave

Feet away falsely fallen watching a breathing into hot earth neck
taking rocks back sodden in blood lapping the pebbles up arches
arches groans. Hazel yes roll wildly in his skull bright opaque catch
on Hal's face. Hal speaking voice low cracks dips blue casting down
deep the cheekbone stain purple and blue. Kneels the blood backed
up the dirt beneath slicks up to catch on teeth cresting out over lips
fevered blue plead. Catch the glean in Hal's eyes swallowing the
ebbing gaze heated rush surface of salt water fear at all's possible
rising off flesh and land all that awaits. Blood down neck Hal's eyes
up, reaching down. Then Hotspur settles loses buck and rear and
rests to the wet of blood and dust prone a hand held over and closing
eyes Hotspur's lips breaks the favors in a long tear and lets them fall
Hal bent throat low and broken to the ground.

O Harry, thou has robbed me of my youth

Henry IV Part 1, V.ii.

[A Variety of Exile]

They are so far away, so far, from the rest, from the guards of
loss. Grounds like concrete and brittle green fingers from a sprawled
paved palm. Loss dense as a gap-mouthed blanks of three flats, flat,
never ending, the sleek, sharp shock of a steel bridge, it's collections of
skin.

No, wait, we're not there yet.

Or we have left it behind.

No, wait, you should know.

Hotspur never leaves behind. Even today, trying to be cavalry. A
cavalry who waits, a dream because to be cavalry means the space in the
first place, the tether or constant loyalty to no one (No one forgets, Hal,
how it was all of your men (*babies!*) who let you win at Calais). And of
course, now, Hotspur tries.

Well, and good, or all well
and good (or no, you idiot, of course not)
yet Hotspur over the next hill because. Because.

There's a joke in their throat.

Because somehow, Hal is behind.

Those wars have past, dear ones. They have to have had. And
Hotspur, fled, but you get to decide

the hows

after the whys.

They ride abreast now, the rest of the journey ahead of them,
and nightfall too, and one hopes the former before the latter. Hal
always riding, at least in tandem, or pushing against and with and past
competitors, with a rhythm, a bounce. (Hotspur: *that's not the right word
for the way Hal's thighs spin.*)

Flair? Panache? Eagerness, the quick flip to reflect
refract away any shine that may direct at him, doggedly
pumping along. Enthusiasm, or

this is where Hotspur finally landed.

And you, rider?

Oh, the tired tiring trying true earnestness.

Anyway.
Off they go. Go on.
Dusk arriving eventually, carrying wound and song, they vanquish their field. No retreat. This, the breath between lines, a simple scene change. Perhaps we have no idea of the mortal wound. *Esperance.*

Together, the earth is easy. The way we move is easy. When we ride together it is as though we are alone, alone together. What do you remember about your kingdom? Do you remember the warm dust of the track to the coast? How we willed ourselves to set up camp fast, to take off with all the sun that would be left us. What do you remember about the earth? We are always abreast here surrounded by darkness's ease, which is to say, near equinox, on fields cast in darkness and shadow, a space without history or record. You know the lands that are yours. You know the lands, and so you want to share them. Do you remember leading me along the river, along the slick rocks, sun still up - do you remember?

If all the field is yours, let me help you remember. If your mother is cold, is she dead? If you must build castles out of stone, will they forever remain so? Prince, do you have to be born on an auspicious day? Will the day you were born always fill with auspices? I was born under cards like the sun, my tongue like the star, to aspire to be an angel stroking her wrists along the jaw of a lion. Women cast down the boys with wands about me.

When you were born on the earth all the cards were yours. I have seen this become true, the good ones to win, how they slide to you, and your easy pace as you trot your triumph about the board. See, we all know, all the field is yours. Remember? Your cards are the cold: the emperor, the hierophant, the empress - halls of stone, of a ruler's place in the world, of rules, of each person and thing's place.

Up from the south, that's me: the pieces of earth you have no memory, save for mine, save for me. This is no easy distillation, no lazy lieutenant's report, these are the paces of my hips that needed to move, hair heavy and tossed back.

A ruler's place in the world, of rules, of each person and thing's place. Mine is a place in any world my feet will find, mine is a place with warm metal, warm earth. What would you do with a memory like that? Would you fight to hold on? Would you howl to never let it go? To save the memory of riding under a night's warmth, how the hymns sounded, how our languages strengthened our tongues.

As the atlas says   no place I have been known

In spring? There? In March
you ride this field?

Of course my horse. Of course
those fields the exhale walking just close to a reek
plains grass, red dirt, dogs far off
In the early dawn ride off, young
again, a rider with home lands
a kid tearing over the earth barefoot
a kid who can ride bareback
No place except for the dead, and I am
left with scent, legs, how to feel free

March: beware, believe it: the Ides
March, beware they all sang
March could be snow or sun or rain

Would've gone it alone. And expected as much.
Ides are the days to pay debts
I wasn't scared. My dirt. It was only ever a place to find heroics.
I carried you. And what else would I do?

Spring, now, and the light in this stretch
of land stretches from your birthpoint to that
point of my blood, the same spring as it will always go.

A Variety of Exile

Carried you said
didn't need anyone
to know it don't
need to tell you

Each field
remember
you were there

What else would
What to be done

All of it is yours
the land of your
birth or exile
stretched here
to the far point
of my own blood
the same spring
as it will go

Would have rode
on alone
knew as much

It is said to be spring now.
The roads closed to me,
ice over rock, a purgatory.

say you so?

Just camp, that night, not enough light to ride. A king's quiet will never feel quite right. But I tried, if unable to be small, to be light. All I was was weight. You stopped trying to be heroic. You had proven yourself a king, you had no need. No need for carry or keep. It was not cold in the wood, and my body could give you nothing. In the night in those trees, fealty meant so little with our broken sleep. Lights on the road, but in exile, together, beyond anyone's care.

In the sun you had called me an errand boy and I smiled and you smiled back, warmed me, warmly.

I wonder, if I was smaller, if I would've known not to carry you, a chest light and empty and delicate, a body ready, mostly eager, for flight. This is what I have lived, all my life. If only these wounds would free this weight. If only there was something to forgive, and I could unbind their openings.

In the morning we rode and you triumphed in the dawn above me. Until the road had to become yours again. Until I once again knew not when the exile would end.

We happy few

Climbing the stones
of Agincourt, your bones
breathe in
the palms

All the women sleep
the spine, her walls.

Kindness is the worst code yet here we are.
Yet a lady's laugh, their softness about you
their clucks and aches at your wounds but
oh to be kind, why, the hardest sort of hope
to have a knife and carve the sweet self out
a hope a charm, I wish to wish you well
I wish I was not a kind
front line of hope that I could
cavalry in with oxygen, with blood that
only continues to thin, each piece out
outlined in ink so thin, lean, and I would say
the weight would leave me free
but there is only a mandate to give
if honor is air, kindness is weight:
a shield, at times, a sword to fight,
a blanket to keep, a song sweet.
Do not say how to paint it this way,
kindness, mine, for me, let me ride off,
away, retreat, Christ, let me be.

And shall it in more shame be further spoken,
That you are

              fool'd, discarded and shook off
By him for whom these shames ye underwent?
No;

      yet time serves wherein you may redeem
Your banish'd honours and restore yourselves

      Into the good thoughts of the world again

Henry IV Part 1, I.iii

would it surprise you to know
hotspur sings?

in an exile there is sun

flight, not flee

somewhere a prince climbs
another breach
these streets
hotspur's hips
canter free

fortunate exile
forward, onward
moving

remember before all this
you had the sea

Notes

Excerpts from *Esperance ma Comforte* have been published in
The Best American Experimental Writing 2014 and *Frighten the
Horses*

Thank you for the care, keeping, and loyalty to these words—Heather, Julie, Liz, and Yana—and thank you, for a lifetime, to Truong for the fortune of an exile.

CARMEN A. AIKEN is a writer in Chicago, whose work has been published in *The Best American Experimental Writing*, *.them*, *Welcome to Hell World*, and a small collection of essays, *In Which There Are Things I've Never Liked Explaining*.